Introduction

Welcome to the wonderful world of sushi! Whether you're a seasoned sushi connoisseur or just starting to explore the delicious flavors of Japanese cuisine, this cookbook is for you. Sushi is not just about raw fish, it's a versatile dish that can be customized to suit any taste and preference. In this cookbook, you'll find a wide range of sushi recipes, from traditional classics to modern fusion rolls, as well as vegetarian and vegan options. Learn how to make perfect sushi rice, prepare fresh seafood, and master the art of rolling your own sushi. With step-by-step instructions and beautiful photos, this cookbook is the ultimate guide to creating restaurant-quality sushi at home. So get ready to explore the flavors and techniques of Japanese cuisine and discover the joy of making sushi in your own kitchen!

California Roll

Ingredients:

4 sheets of sushi nori (seaweed)
2 cups sushi rice (short-grain Japanese rice)
1 avocado, ripe and sliced
1/2 cucumber, seeded and cut into thin strips
8 imitation crab sticks, shredded or cut into strips
Soy sauce, for dipping
Pickled ginger, for serving
Wasabi, for serving
Sesame seeds (optional), for garnish

Instructions:

Cook the sushi rice according to the package instructions. Once cooked, let it cool to room temperature.
Place a bamboo sushi rolling mat on a flat surface and cover it with plastic wrap. This will prevent the rice from sticking to the mat.
Lay one sheet of nori on the rolling mat. Wet your hands with water to prevent the rice from sticking to them, and take a handful of sushi rice. Spread the rice evenly over the nori, leaving a 1-inch gap at the top.
Sprinkle sesame seeds (if using) over the rice. Flip the nori sheet over so that the rice side is facing down.
Arrange slices of avocado, cucumber strips, and shredded crab sticks in a line along the bottom edge of the nori sheet.
Lift the bottom edge of the bamboo mat and start rolling it tightly, using your fingers to hold the fillings in place. Apply gentle pressure to ensure a tight roll.
Continue rolling until the entire sheet of nori is wrapped around the fillings. Dampen the top edge of the nori sheet with water to seal the roll.
Repeat the process with the remaining nori sheets and ingredients.
Use a sharp knife to slice each roll into bite-sized pieces. Dip the knife in water or vinegar between each cut to prevent sticking.
Serve the California rolls with soy sauce, pickled ginger, and wasabi on the side.
Enjoy your homemade California Roll!

Spicy Tuna Roll

Ingredients:

4 sheets of sushi nori (seaweed)
2 cups sushi rice (short-grain Japanese rice)
1/2 lb fresh tuna, finely chopped or minced
2 tablespoons mayonnaise
1 tablespoon Sriracha sauce (adjust to your preferred level of spiciness)
1/2 cucumber, seeded and cut into thin strips
Soy sauce, for dipping
Pickled ginger, for serving
Wasabi, for serving
Sesame seeds (optional), for garnish

Instructions:

Cook the sushi rice according to the package instructions. Once cooked, let it cool to room temperature.
In a bowl, mix together the finely chopped tuna, mayonnaise, and Sriracha sauce until well combined. Adjust the amount of Sriracha sauce according to your desired level of spiciness.
Place a bamboo sushi rolling mat on a flat surface and cover it with plastic wrap.
Lay one sheet of nori on the rolling mat. Wet your hands with water to prevent the rice from sticking to them, and take a handful of sushi rice. Spread the rice evenly over the nori, leaving a 1-inch gap at the top.
Sprinkle sesame seeds (if using) over the rice. Flip the nori sheet over so that the rice side is facing down.
Spread a thin layer of the spicy tuna mixture along the bottom edge of the nori sheet.
Arrange cucumber strips on top of the spicy tuna mixture.
Lift the bottom edge of the bamboo mat and start rolling it tightly, using your fingers to hold the fillings in place. Apply gentle pressure to ensure a tight roll.
Continue rolling until the entire sheet of nori is wrapped around the fillings. Dampen the top edge of the nori sheet with water to seal the roll.
Repeat the process with the remaining nori sheets and ingredients.
Use a sharp knife to slice each roll into bite-sized pieces. Dip the knife in water or vinegar between each cut to prevent sticking.
Serve the Spicy Tuna Rolls with soy sauce, pickled ginger, and wasabi on the side.
Enjoy your homemade Spicy Tuna Rolls!

Spicy Crab Roll

Ingredients:

4 sheets of sushi nori (seaweed)
2 cups sushi rice (short-grain Japanese rice)
1/2 lb imitation crab meat, shredded
2 tablespoons mayonnaise
1 tablespoon Sriracha sauce (adjust to your preferred level of spiciness)
1/2 cucumber, seeded and cut into thin strips
Soy sauce, for dipping
Pickled ginger, for serving
Wasabi, for serving
Sesame seeds (optional), for garnish

Instructions:

Cook the sushi rice according to the package instructions. Once cooked, let it cool to room temperature.
In a bowl, mix together the shredded imitation crab meat, mayonnaise, and Sriracha sauce until well combined. Adjust the amount of Sriracha sauce according to your desired level of spiciness.
Place a bamboo sushi rolling mat on a flat surface and cover it with plastic wrap.
Lay one sheet of nori on the rolling mat. Wet your hands with water to prevent the rice from sticking to them, and take a handful of sushi rice. Spread the rice evenly over the nori, leaving a 1-inch gap at the top.
Sprinkle sesame seeds (if using) over the rice. Flip the nori sheet over so that the rice side is facing down.
Spread a thin layer of the spicy crab mixture along the bottom edge of the nori sheet.
Arrange cucumber strips on top of the spicy crab mixture.
Lift the bottom edge of the bamboo mat and start rolling it tightly, using your fingers to hold the fillings in place. Apply gentle pressure to ensure a tight roll.
Continue rolling until the entire sheet of nori is wrapped around the fillings. Dampen the top edge of the nori sheet with water to seal the roll.
Repeat the process with the remaining nori sheets and ingredients.
Use a sharp knife to slice each roll into bite-sized pieces. Dip the knife in water or vinegar between each cut to prevent sticking.
Serve the Spicy Crab Rolls with soy sauce, pickled ginger, and wasabi on the side.
Enjoy your homemade Spicy Crab Rolls!

Sushi Rice

Ingredients:

2 cups sushi rice (short-grain Japanese rice)
2 cups water
1/4 cup rice vinegar
2 tablespoons sugar
1 teaspoon salt

Instructions:

Rinse the sushi rice in cold water until the water runs clear. This helps to remove excess starch from the rice.

In a saucepan, combine the rinsed rice and water. Let the rice soak in the water for 30 minutes. After soaking, bring the rice to a boil over medium heat. Once boiling, reduce the heat to low, cover the saucepan with a tight-fitting lid, and simmer for about 15-20 minutes or until the rice is tender and the water is absorbed.

While the rice is cooking, prepare the sushi vinegar mixture. In a small saucepan, heat the rice vinegar, sugar, and salt over low heat until the sugar and salt dissolve. Stir occasionally.

Once the rice is cooked, transfer it to a large mixing bowl or a wooden sushi rice tub (hangiri). Gradually pour the sushi vinegar mixture over the rice while gently folding and mixing it with a wooden spatula or a rice paddle.

Continue folding and mixing the rice until the vinegar mixture is evenly distributed and absorbed by the rice. Be careful not to overmix, as it can make the rice mushy.

Let the seasoned sushi rice cool to room temperature before using it for sushi rolls or nigiri sushi. You can fan the rice or use a handheld fan to help cool it down more quickly.

Once the sushi rice is cooled, it's ready to be used in your favorite sushi recipes. Enjoy your homemade sushi rice!

Shrimp Tempura Rolls

Ingredients:

4 sheets of sushi nori (seaweed)
2 cups sushi rice (short-grain Japanese rice)
8 large shrimp, peeled and deveined
1 cup all-purpose flour
1/2 cup cornstarch
1 teaspoon baking powder
1 cup ice-cold water
Vegetable oil, for frying
1/2 cucumber, seeded and cut into thin strips
Soy sauce, for dipping
Pickled ginger, for serving
Wasabi, for serving

Instructions:

Cook the sushi rice according to the package instructions. Once cooked, let it cool to room temperature.
Prepare the tempura batter by combining the all-purpose flour, cornstarch, and baking powder in a bowl.
Gradually whisk in the ice-cold water until the batter is smooth and has a slightly thick consistency.
Heat vegetable oil in a deep pan or pot to about 350°F (175°C).
Dip the shrimp into the tempura batter, making sure they are well coated.
Carefully place the battered shrimp into the hot oil and fry until they turn golden brown and crispy.
Remove the shrimp from the oil and let them drain on a paper towel-lined plate.
Place a bamboo sushi rolling mat on a flat surface and cover it with plastic wrap.
Lay one sheet of nori on the rolling mat. Wet your hands with water to prevent the rice from sticking to them, and take a handful of sushi rice. Spread the rice evenly over the nori, leaving a 1-inch gap at the top.
Place a line of cucumber strips along the bottom edge of the nori sheet.
Arrange the cooked shrimp on top of the cucumber strips.
Lift the bottom edge of the bamboo mat and start rolling it tightly, using your fingers to hold the fillings in place. Apply gentle pressure to ensure a tight roll.
Continue rolling until the entire sheet of nori is wrapped around the fillings. Dampen the top edge of the nori sheet with water to seal the roll.
Repeat the process with the remaining nori sheets and ingredients.
Use a sharp knife to slice each roll into bite-sized pieces. Dip the knife in water or vinegar between each cut to prevent sticking.
Serve the Shrimp Tempura Rolls with soy sauce, pickled ginger, and wasabi on the side.
Enjoy your homemade Shrimp Tempura Rolls!

Chirashi Bowls

Ingredients:

2 cups sushi rice (short-grain Japanese rice)
2 tablespoons rice vinegar
1 tablespoon sugar
1 teaspoon salt
Assorted sashimi (such as tuna, salmon, yellowtail, etc.), sliced into bite-sized pieces
Assorted vegetables (such as cucumber, avocado, radish, etc.), thinly sliced or diced
Nori sheets, cut into thin strips
Pickled ginger, for serving
Wasabi, for serving
Soy sauce, for serving
Sesame seeds (optional), for garnish
Green onions (optional), sliced for garnish

Instructions:

Cook the sushi rice according to the package instructions. Once cooked, let it cool to room temperature.

In a small bowl, mix together the rice vinegar, sugar, and salt until the sugar and salt dissolve.

Transfer the cooked rice to a large mixing bowl and pour the vinegar mixture over it. Gently fold and mix the rice with a wooden spatula or rice paddle, being careful not to crush the grains. Keep mixing until the vinegar is evenly distributed and absorbed by the rice.

Divide the seasoned sushi rice among serving bowls or plates.

Arrange the sliced sashimi and assorted vegetables on top of the rice in an aesthetically pleasing manner.

Garnish with nori strips, pickled ginger, and sesame seeds (if desired).

Serve the Chirashi Bowls with soy sauce and wasabi on the side. You can drizzle a little soy sauce over the toppings if desired.

Optionally, garnish with sliced green onions for added flavor and presentation.

Enjoy your homemade Chirashi Bowls, a beautiful and delicious sushi-inspired dish!

Boston Roll

Ingredients:

4 sheets of sushi nori (seaweed)
2 cups sushi rice (short-grain Japanese rice)
8 oz cooked lobster meat, chopped
1/2 cup mayonnaise
1 tablespoon lemon juice
1/2 avocado, sliced
1/2 cucumber, seeded and cut into thin strips
Soy sauce, for dipping
Pickled ginger, for serving
Wasabi, for serving

Instructions:

Cook the sushi rice according to the package instructions. Once cooked, let it cool to room temperature.
In a bowl, mix together the chopped lobster meat, mayonnaise, and lemon juice until well combined. This will be the lobster salad filling for the Boston Roll.
Place a bamboo sushi rolling mat on a flat surface and cover it with plastic wrap.
Lay one sheet of nori on the rolling mat. Wet your hands with water to prevent the rice from sticking to them, and take a handful of sushi rice. Spread the rice evenly over the nori, leaving a 1-inch gap at the top.
Spread a thin layer of the lobster salad along the bottom edge of the nori sheet.
Arrange slices of avocado and cucumber strips on top of the lobster salad.
Lift the bottom edge of the bamboo mat and start rolling it tightly, using your fingers to hold the fillings in place. Apply gentle pressure to ensure a tight roll.
Continue rolling until the entire sheet of nori is wrapped around the fillings. Dampen the top edge of the nori sheet with water to seal the roll.
Repeat the process with the remaining nori sheets and ingredients.
Use a sharp knife to slice each roll into bite-sized pieces. Dip the knife in water or vinegar between each cut to prevent sticking.
Serve the Boston Rolls with soy sauce, pickled ginger, and wasabi on the side.
Enjoy your homemade Boston Rolls, a delicious combination of lobster, avocado, and cucumber!

Dragon Roll

Ingredients:

4 sheets of sushi nori (seaweed)
2 cups sushi rice (short-grain Japanese rice)
8 oz cooked eel or unagi, sliced into thin strips
1/2 avocado, sliced
1/2 cucumber, seeded and cut into thin strips
4 oz cream cheese, sliced into thin strips
Soy sauce, for dipping
Eel sauce or unagi sauce, for drizzling
Sesame seeds (optional), for garnish
Pickled ginger, for serving
Wasabi, for serving

Instructions:

Cook the sushi rice according to the package instructions. Once cooked, let it cool to room temperature. Place a bamboo sushi rolling mat on a flat surface and cover it with plastic wrap.
Lay one sheet of nori on the rolling mat. Wet your hands with water to prevent the rice from sticking to them, and take a handful of sushi rice. Spread the rice evenly over the nori, leaving a 1-inch gap at the top.
Sprinkle sesame seeds (if using) over the rice. Flip the nori sheet over so that the rice side is facing down.
Arrange slices of eel, avocado, cucumber, and cream cheese along the bottom edge of the nori sheet.
Lift the bottom edge of the bamboo mat and start rolling it tightly, using your fingers to hold the fillings in place. Apply gentle pressure to ensure a tight roll.
Continue rolling until the entire sheet of nori is wrapped around the fillings. Dampen the top edge of the nori sheet with water to seal the roll.
Repeat the process with the remaining nori sheets and ingredients.
Use a sharp knife to slice each roll into bite-sized pieces. Dip the knife in water or vinegar between each cut to prevent sticking.
Arrange the Dragon Roll pieces on a serving platter, arranging them to resemble a dragon with the eel and avocado on top.
Drizzle eel sauce or unagi sauce over the Dragon Roll pieces.
Serve the Dragon Rolls with soy sauce, pickled ginger, and wasabi on the side.
Enjoy your homemade Dragon Rolls, an impressive and delicious sushi creation!

Rainbow Roll

Ingredients:

4 sheets of sushi nori (seaweed)
2 cups sushi rice (short-grain Japanese rice)
Assorted sashimi (such as tuna, salmon, yellowtail, etc.), thinly sliced into strips
1/2 avocado, sliced
1/2 cucumber, seeded and cut into thin strips
Soy sauce, for dipping
Pickled ginger, for serving
Wasabi, for serving

Instructions:

Cook the sushi rice according to the package instructions. Once cooked, let it cool to room temperature.
Place a bamboo sushi rolling mat on a flat surface and cover it with plastic wrap.
Lay one sheet of nori on the rolling mat. Wet your hands with water to prevent the rice from sticking to them, and take a handful of sushi rice. Spread the rice evenly over the nori, leaving a 1-inch gap at the top.
Flip the nori sheet over so that the rice side is facing down.
Arrange thin strips of assorted sashimi (tuna, salmon, yellowtail, etc.) in a row along the bottom edge of the nori sheet.
Place a line of cucumber strips on top of the sashimi.
Lift the bottom edge of the bamboo mat and start rolling it tightly, using your fingers to hold the fillings in place. Apply gentle pressure to ensure a tight roll.
Continue rolling until the entire sheet of nori is wrapped around the fillings. Dampen the top edge of the nori sheet with water to seal the roll.
Repeat the process with the remaining nori sheets and ingredients.
Use a sharp knife to slice each roll into bite-sized pieces. Dip the knife in water or vinegar between each cut to prevent sticking.
Arrange the Rainbow Roll pieces on a serving platter, placing them in a colorful pattern with different sashimi toppings visible on each piece.
Serve the Rainbow Rolls with soy sauce, pickled ginger, and wasabi on the side.
Enjoy your homemade Rainbow Rolls, a vibrant and delicious sushi delight!

Philadelphia Roll

Ingredients:

4 sheets of sushi nori (seaweed)
2 cups sushi rice (short-grain Japanese rice)
4 oz smoked salmon, sliced into thin strips
4 oz cream cheese, sliced into thin strips
1/2 cucumber, seeded and cut into thin strips
Soy sauce, for dipping
Pickled ginger, for serving
Wasabi, for serving

Instructions:

Cook the sushi rice according to the package instructions. Once cooked, let it cool to room temperature.
Place a bamboo sushi rolling mat on a flat surface and cover it with plastic wrap.
Lay one sheet of nori on the rolling mat. Wet your hands with water to prevent the rice from sticking to them, and take a handful of sushi rice. Spread the rice evenly over the nori, leaving a 1-inch gap at the top.
Flip the nori sheet over so that the rice side is facing down.
Arrange slices of smoked salmon, cream cheese, and cucumber strips along the bottom edge of the nori sheet.
Lift the bottom edge of the bamboo mat and start rolling it tightly, using your fingers to hold the fillings in place. Apply gentle pressure to ensure a tight roll.
Continue rolling until the entire sheet of nori is wrapped around the fillings. Dampen the top edge of the nori sheet with water to seal the roll.
Repeat the process with the remaining nori sheets and ingredients.
Use a sharp knife to slice each roll into bite-sized pieces. Dip the knife in water or vinegar between each cut to prevent sticking.
Arrange the Philadelphia Roll pieces on a serving platter.
Serve the Philadelphia Rolls with soy sauce, pickled ginger, and wasabi on the side.
Enjoy your homemade Philadelphia Rolls, a delicious combination of smoked salmon, cream cheese, and cucumber!

Sushi Stacks

Ingredients:

2 cups sushi rice (short-grain Japanese rice)
2 tablespoons rice vinegar
1 tablespoon sugar
1 teaspoon salt
Assorted sushi fillings (such as diced raw fish, cooked shrimp, avocado, cucumber, etc.)
Soy sauce, for drizzling
Pickled ginger, for serving
Wasabi, for serving
Optional toppings: sesame seeds, scallions, nori strips, etc.

Instructions:

Cook the sushi rice according to the package instructions. Once cooked, let it cool to room temperature.
In a small bowl, mix together the rice vinegar, sugar, and salt until the sugar and salt dissolve.
Transfer the cooked rice to a large mixing bowl and pour the vinegar mixture over it. Gently fold and mix the rice with a wooden spatula or rice paddle, being careful not to crush the grains. Keep mixing until the vinegar is evenly distributed and absorbed by the rice.
Prepare your desired sushi fillings by dicing them into small, bite-sized pieces.
Take a small, round food ring or mold and place it on a plate. Alternatively, you can use a clean, empty can with both ends removed.
Fill the mold with a layer of sushi rice, pressing it down gently with a spoon or your fingers to create a compact base.
Add a layer of your desired sushi fillings on top of the rice layer.
Add another layer of sushi rice on top of the fillings, pressing it down gently.
Carefully lift the mold or can off the plate, leaving the sushi stack intact.
Repeat the process to make additional sushi stacks with different fillings or combinations.
Drizzle soy sauce over the sushi stacks.
Optionally, sprinkle sesame seeds, sliced scallions, or nori strips on top for added flavor and presentation.
Serve the Sushi Stacks with pickled ginger and wasabi on the side.
Enjoy your homemade Sushi Stacks, a creative and delicious twist on traditional sushi presentations!

Kimbap

Ingredients:

4 cups cooked short-grain white rice
4 sheets of roasted seaweed (gim/nori)
8 ounces cooked and seasoned bulgogi beef or any desired protein (sliced into thin strips)
1 carrot, julienned
1 cucumber, julienned
4 eggs, beaten and cooked into a thin omelette
1 tablespoon vegetable oil
Salt, to taste
Sesame oil, for brushing
Soy sauce, for dipping

Optional fillings:

Pickled radish (danmuji)
Spinach, blanched and seasoned with sesame oil and salt
Crab meat (imitation or real)
Avocado, sliced
Kimchi

Instructions:

In a skillet, heat the vegetable oil over medium heat. Add the julienned carrot and cucumber, and sauté for a few minutes until they soften slightly. Season with a pinch of salt. Set aside.
In the same skillet, cook the beaten eggs into a thin omelette. Once cooked, remove from the heat and slice it into thin strips. Set aside.
Lay a bamboo sushi rolling mat on a flat surface and place a sheet of roasted seaweed (gim/nori) on top.
Wet your hands with water to prevent the rice from sticking to them. Take a handful of cooked rice and spread it evenly over the seaweed, leaving a small border at the top.
Arrange the desired fillings (such as bulgogi beef, sautéed vegetables, sliced omelette, pickled radish, etc.) in a line across the center of the rice.
Using the bamboo mat, roll the seaweed tightly over the fillings, applying gentle pressure to create a compact roll. Moisten the top border of the seaweed with water to seal the roll.
Repeat the process to make additional rolls with the remaining ingredients.
Brush the rolls with sesame oil to add flavor and shine.
Using a sharp knife, slice each roll into bite-sized pieces.
Serve the Kimbap with soy sauce for dipping.
Enjoy your homemade Kimbap, a delicious and satisfying Korean dish!

Cucumber Sushi

Ingredients:

2 cups sushi rice (short-grain Japanese rice)
4 sheets of sushi nori (seaweed)
1 large cucumber
Soy sauce, for dipping
Pickled ginger, for serving
Wasabi, for serving

Instructions:

Cook the sushi rice according to the package instructions. Once cooked, let it cool to room temperature.
Peel the cucumber and slice it lengthwise into thin, long strips. You can use a mandoline slicer or a vegetable peeler to achieve thin slices.
Place a bamboo sushi rolling mat on a flat surface and cover it with plastic wrap.
Lay one sheet of nori on the rolling mat. Wet your hands with water to prevent the rice from sticking to them, and take a handful of sushi rice. Spread the rice evenly over the nori, leaving a 1-inch gap at the top.\
Place cucumber slices along the bottom edge of the nori sheet.
Lift the bottom edge of the bamboo mat and start rolling it tightly, using your fingers to hold the fillings in place. Apply gentle pressure to ensure a tight roll.
Continue rolling until the entire sheet of nori is wrapped around the cucumber filling. Dampen the top edge of the nori sheet with water to seal the roll.
Repeat the process with the remaining nori sheets and ingredients.
Use a sharp knife to slice each roll into bite-sized pieces. Dip the knife in water or vinegar between each cut to prevent sticking.
Arrange the Cucumber Sushi pieces on a serving platter.
Serve the Cucumber Sushi with soy sauce, pickled ginger, and wasabi on the side.
Enjoy your homemade Cucumber Sushi, a light and refreshing option perfect for sushi lovers!

Cauliflower Sushi Stacks

Ingredients:

4 cups riced cauliflower (store-bought or homemade)
2 tablespoons rice vinegar
1 tablespoon sugar
1 teaspoon salt
Assorted sushi fillings (such as diced raw fish, cooked shrimp, avocado, cucumber, etc.)
Soy sauce, for drizzling
Pickled ginger, for serving
Wasabi, for serving
Optional toppings: sesame seeds, scallions, nori strips, etc

Instructions:

If using fresh cauliflower, grate it or pulse it in a food processor until it resembles rice. If using store-bought riced cauliflower, skip this step.
In a small bowl, mix together the rice vinegar, sugar, and salt until the sugar and salt dissolve.
Place the riced cauliflower in a microwave-safe bowl and microwave it on high for 5 minutes, or until cooked and tender.
Transfer the cooked cauliflower rice to a large mixing bowl and pour the vinegar mixture over it. Gently fold and mix the cauliflower rice with a fork or spoon, ensuring the vinegar is evenly distributed.
Prepare your desired sushi fillings by dicing them into small, bite-sized pieces.
Take a small, round food ring or mold and place it on a plate. Alternatively, you can use a clean, empty can with both ends removed.
Fill the mold with a layer of cauliflower rice, pressing it down gently with a spoon or your fingers to create a compact base.
Add a layer of your desired sushi fillings on top of the cauliflower rice layer.
Add another layer of cauliflower rice on top of the fillings, pressing it down gently.
Carefully lift the mold or can off the plate, leaving the cauliflower sushi stack intact.
Repeat the process to make additional cauliflower sushi stacks with different fillings or combinations.
Optionally, sprinkle sesame seeds, sliced scallions, or nori strips on top for added flavor and presentation.\
Serve the Cauliflower Sushi Stacks with soy sauce, pickled ginger, and wasabi on the side.
Enjoy your homemade Cauliflower Sushi Stacks, a delicious and healthier alternative to traditional sushi rolls!

NEW YORK ROLL

Ingredients:

4 sheets of sushi nori (seaweed)
2 cups sushi rice (short-grain Japanese rice)
8 ounces fresh salmon, thinly sliced
4 ounces cream cheese, cut into thin strips
1 ripe avocado, sliced
Soy sauce, for dipping
Pickled ginger, for serving
Wasabi, for serving

Instructions:

Cook the sushi rice according to the package instructions. Once cooked, let it cool to room temperature.
Place a bamboo sushi rolling mat on a flat surface and cover it with plastic wrap.
Lay one sheet of nori on the rolling mat. Wet your hands with water to prevent the rice from sticking to them, and take a handful of sushi rice. Spread the rice evenly over the nori, leaving a 1-inch gap at the top.
Flip the nori sheet over so that the rice side is facing down.
Place slices of fresh salmon along the bottom edge of the nori sheet.
Arrange strips of cream cheese and avocado slices on top of the salmon.
Lift the bottom edge of the bamboo mat and start rolling it tightly, using your fingers to hold the fillings in place. Apply gentle pressure to ensure a tight roll.
Continue rolling until the entire sheet of nori is wrapped around the fillings. Dampen the top edge of the nori sheet with water to seal the roll.
Repeat the process with the remaining nori sheets and ingredients.
Use a sharp knife to slice each roll into bite-sized pieces. Dip the knife in water or vinegar between each cut to prevent sticking.
Arrange the New York Roll pieces on a serving platter.
Serve the New York Rolls with soy sauce, pickled ginger, and wasabi on the side.
Enjoy your homemade New York Rolls, a delicious combination of salmon, avocado, and cream cheese!

SALMON ROLL

Ingredients:

4 sheets of sushi nori (seaweed)
2 cups sushi rice (short-grain Japanese rice)
8 ounces fresh salmon, thinly sliced
1/2 cucumber, julienned
Soy sauce, for dipping
Pickled ginger, for serving
Wasabi, for serving

Instructions:

Cook the sushi rice according to the package instructions. Once cooked, let it cool to room temperature.
Place a bamboo sushi rolling mat on a flat surface and cover it with plastic wrap.
Lay one sheet of nori on the rolling mat. Wet your hands with water to prevent the rice from sticking to them, and take a handful of sushi rice. Spread the rice evenly over the nori, leaving a 1-inch gap at the top.
Flip the nori sheet over so that the rice side is facing down.
Place slices of fresh salmon and julienned cucumber along the bottom edge of the nori sheet.
Lift the bottom edge of the bamboo mat and start rolling it tightly, using your fingers to hold the fillings in place. Apply gentle pressure to ensure a tight roll.
Continue rolling until the entire sheet of nori is wrapped around the fillings. Dampen the top edge of the nori sheet with water to seal the roll.
Repeat the process with the remaining nori sheets and ingredients.
Use a sharp knife to slice each roll into bite-sized pieces. Dip the knife in water or vinegar between each cut to prevent sticking.
Arrange the Salmon Roll pieces on a serving platter.
Serve the Salmon Rolls with soy sauce, pickled ginger, and wasabi on the side.
Enjoy your homemade Salmon Rolls, a flavorful and satisfying sushi choice!

SPICY TUNA ROLL

Ingredients:

4 sheets of sushi nori (seaweed)
2 cups sushi rice (short-grain Japanese rice)
8 ounces fresh tuna, finely chopped or minced
2 tablespoons mayonnaise
1 tablespoon Sriracha sauce (adjust according to your preferred level of spiciness)
1/2 cucumber, julienned
Soy sauce, for dipping
Pickled ginger, for serving
Wasabi, for serving

Instructions:

In a small bowl, mix together the chopped tuna, mayonnaise, and Sriracha sauce until well combined. Adjust the amount of Sriracha to achieve your desired level of spiciness.
Place a bamboo sushi rolling mat on a flat surface and cover it with plastic wrap.
Lay one sheet of nori on the rolling mat. Wet your hands with water to prevent the rice from sticking to them, and take a handful of sushi rice. Spread the rice evenly over the nori, leaving a 1-inch gap at the top.
Flip the nori sheet over so that the rice side is facing down.
Spread a thin layer of the spicy tuna mixture along the bottom edge of the nori sheet.
Place julienned cucumber on top of the spicy tuna mixture.
Lift the bottom edge of the bamboo mat and start rolling it tightly, using your fingers to hold the fillings in place. Apply gentle pressure to ensure a tight roll.
Continue rolling until the entire sheet of nori is wrapped around the fillings. Dampen the top edge of the nori sheet with water to seal the roll.
Repeat the process with the remaining nori sheets and ingredients.
Use a sharp knife to slice each roll into bite-sized pieces. Dip the knife in water or vinegar between each cut to prevent sticking.
Arrange the Spicy Tuna Roll pieces on a serving platter.
Serve the Spicy Tuna Rolls with soy sauce, pickled ginger, and wasabi on the side.
Enjoy your homemade Spicy Tuna Rolls, a flavorful and fiery sushi delight!

NATTO ROLL

Ingredients:

4 sheets of sushi nori (seaweed)
2 cups sushi rice (short-grain Japanese rice)
1 package of natto (fermented soybeans)
1 tablespoon soy sauce
1 teaspoon sesame oil
1/2 cucumber, julienned
Pickled ginger, for serving
Wasabi, for serving

Instructions:

Cook the sushi rice according to the package instructions. Once cooked, let it cool to room temperature.
In a small bowl, mix the natto with soy sauce and sesame oil. Stir well to combine.
Place a bamboo sushi rolling mat on a flat surface and cover it with plastic wrap.
Lay one sheet of nori on the rolling mat. Wet your hands with water to prevent the rice from sticking to them, and take a handful of sushi rice. Spread the rice evenly over the nori, leaving a 1-inch gap at the top.
Flip the nori sheet over so that the rice side is facing down.
Spread the natto mixture along the bottom edge of the nori sheet.
Place julienned cucumber on top of the natto mixture.
Lift the bottom edge of the bamboo mat and start rolling it tightly, using your fingers to hold the fillings in place. Apply gentle pressure to ensure a tight roll.
Continue rolling until the entire sheet of nori is wrapped around the fillings. Dampen the top edge of the nori sheet with water to seal the roll.
Repeat the process with the remaining nori sheets and ingredients.
Use a sharp knife to slice each roll into bite-sized pieces. Dip the knife in water or vinegar between each cut to prevent sticking.
Arrange the Natto Rolls on a serving platter.
Serve the Natto Rolls with pickled ginger and wasabi on the side.
Enjoy your homemade Natto Rolls, a unique and flavorful sushi option!

Nigiri

Nigiri is a classic type of sushi that consists of a small hand-formed mound of sushi rice topped with a slice of raw or cooked seafood. Here's a general recipe for making Nigiri:

Ingredients:

Sushi rice (short-grain Japanese rice)
Fresh seafood (such as salmon, tuna, shrimp, eel, etc.)
Soy sauce, for dipping
Wasabi, for serving
Pickled ginger, for serving

Instructions:

Cook the sushi rice according to the package instructions. Once cooked, let it cool to room temperature.

Prepare the seafood by slicing it into thin, bite-sized pieces. You can choose your favorite types of seafood, such as salmon, tuna, shrimp, or eel.

Wet your hands with water to prevent the rice from sticking to them. Take a small handful of sushi rice and gently form it into a compact oval-shaped mound using your palms. The rice should be slightly warm or at room temperature for the best texture.

Place a slice of seafood on top of the rice mound. You can lightly brush the seafood with soy sauce or add a small amount of wasabi between the rice and the seafood for extra flavor if desired.

Repeat the process with the remaining sushi rice and seafood slices until you have made the desired number of nigiri pieces.

Arrange the nigiri on a serving platter.

Serve the nigiri with soy sauce, pickled ginger, and additional wasabi on the side.

Nigiri is typically eaten in one bite, so it's best to pick up a piece with chopsticks, dip it in soy sauce if desired, and enjoy it in a single bite to experience the combination of flavors and textures.

Note: It's important to use fresh, high-quality seafood when making nigiri. If you're unsure about handling raw seafood or sourcing sushi-grade fish, it's recommended to consult with a knowledgeable seafood vendor or sushi chef.

Chirashizushi (Scattered Sushi)

Chirashizushi, also known as "Scattered Sushi," is a colorful and flavorful dish consisting of sushi rice topped with a variety of ingredients. Here's a recipe to make Chirashizushi:

Ingredients:

2 cups sushi rice (short-grain Japanese rice)
4 tablespoons rice vinegar
2 tablespoons sugar
1 teaspoon salt
Assorted toppings (such as sashimi-grade fish, cooked shrimp, tamagoyaki (Japanese rolled omelette), cucumber, avocado, pickled ginger, seaweed, etc.)
Soy sauce, for drizzling
Wasabi, for serving
Pickled ginger, for serving

Instructions:

Cook the sushi rice according to the package instructions. Once cooked, transfer it to a large bowl.

In a small bowl, mix together the rice vinegar, sugar, and salt until the sugar and salt dissolve.

While the rice is still warm, pour the vinegar mixture over the rice. Gently fold and mix the rice using a wooden spatula or rice paddle, ensuring that the vinegar is evenly distributed. Let the rice cool to room temperature.

Prepare your desired toppings by slicing or cutting them into bite-sized pieces. Some popular choices include sashimi-grade fish like salmon, tuna, or yellowtail, cooked shrimp, tamagoyaki (Japanese rolled omelette), cucumber, avocado, pickled ginger, and seaweed.

To assemble the Chirashizushi, place a generous amount of sushi rice in individual bowls or a large serving platter.

Arrange the assorted toppings over the rice, scattering them in an aesthetically pleasing manner.

Serve the Chirashizushi with soy sauce, wasabi, and pickled ginger on the side.

Each person can mix the toppings and rice together before eating, or they can enjoy the toppings separately. Chirashizushi is a versatile dish, and you can customize it with your favorite ingredients to create a beautiful and delicious meal.

Note: The toppings can vary based on personal preference and availability. Ensure that any raw seafood used for sashimi is fresh and of high quality.

Temaki

Temaki, also known as "hand rolls," are cone-shaped sushi rolls that you can easily make at home. Here's a recipe to make Temaki:

Ingredients:

4 sheets of sushi nori (seaweed)
2 cups sushi rice (short-grain Japanese rice)
Assorted fillings (such as sashimi-grade fish, cooked shrimp, cucumber, avocado, carrots, sprouts, etc.)
Soy sauce, for dipping
Wasabi, for serving
Pickled ginger, for serving

Instructions:

Cook the sushi rice according to the package instructions. Once cooked, let it cool to room temperature.
Prepare your desired fillings by slicing them into thin strips. Popular options include sashimi-grade fish like tuna or salmon, cooked shrimp, cucumber, avocado, carrots, sprouts, or any other ingredients you enjoy.
Place a sheet of nori on a clean, dry surface. Wet your hands with water to prevent the rice from sticking to them, and take a handful of sushi rice. Spread the rice diagonally across one corner of the nori sheet, leaving a small border at the edges.
Place your desired fillings on top of the rice, arranging them in a line from one corner to the opposite corner of the nori sheet.
Starting from the rice-covered corner, roll the nori sheet tightly into a cone shape, tucking in the fillings as you go. Seal the edge of the nori sheet by moistening it slightly with water.
Repeat the process with the remaining nori sheets and fillings.
Serve the Temaki rolls immediately with soy sauce, wasabi, and pickled ginger on the side.
Temaki rolls are best enjoyed right away as the nori tends to soften when exposed to moisture from the rice and fillings. You can get creative with your fillings and customize the Temaki rolls to your taste. Enjoy the delicious and interactive experience of making and eating Temaki at home!

Sashimi

Sashimi is a Japanese delicacy consisting of fresh, thinly sliced raw fish or seafood. It is typically served as an appetizer or part of a sushi platter. Here's a basic recipe for sashimi:

Ingredients:

Fresh sashimi-grade fish or seafood (such as tuna, salmon, yellowtail, scallops, etc.)
Soy sauce, for dipping
Wasabi, for serving
Pickled ginger, for serving

Instructions:

Start by ensuring that you have fresh, high-quality sashimi-grade fish or seafood. It's important to source your fish from a reputable fishmonger or Japanese grocery store to ensure it's safe to consume raw.
Begin by carefully cleaning the fish or seafood. Remove any scales, bones, or tough membranes. Rinse it gently under cold water and pat it dry with a paper towel.
Place the fish or seafood on a clean cutting board. Using a sharp, non-serrated knife, slice the fish or seafood into thin, even slices. It's important to slice against the grain for the best texture. Aim for slices that are around 1/4 to 1/2 inch thick.
Arrange the sashimi slices on a serving platter or individual plates. You can be creative with the presentation by overlapping the slices or arranging them in an aesthetically pleasing manner.
Serve the sashimi with soy sauce, wasabi, and pickled ginger on the side. Traditionally, a small amount of wasabi is mixed into the soy sauce as a dipping sauce. Use chopsticks to dip the sashimi slices into the soy sauce and enjoy.
Note: It's important to handle raw seafood with care and follow proper food safety guidelines. Ensure that you're using fresh, sashimi-grade fish or seafood from reliable sources. If you're unsure about handling raw fish, it's recommended to consult with a knowledgeable fishmonger or sushi chef.

Salmon and Avocado Temari Sushi

Temari Sushi is a type of sushi that consists of small, bite-sized sushi balls formed by hand. They are often beautifully decorated and can feature various toppings and fillings. Here are two recipes for Temari Sushi:

Ingredients:

Sushi rice (short-grain Japanese rice)
Fresh salmon, thinly sliced
Ripe avocado, thinly sliced
Nori (seaweed), cut into thin strips
Soy sauce, for dipping
Wasabi, for serving
Pickled ginger, for serving

Instructions:
Prepare the sushi rice by cooking it according to the package instructions. Once cooked, let it cool to room temperature.
Wet your hands with water to prevent the rice from sticking. Take a small amount of sushi rice and shape it into a compact ball using your palms. The rice ball should be around 1-2 inches in diameter.
Place a slice of salmon on top of the rice ball, slightly overlapping it.
Add a slice of avocado on top of the salmon.
Use a strip of nori to wrap around the sides of the rice ball, securing the salmon and avocado in place.
Repeat the process with the remaining ingredients to make more Temari Sushi balls.
Arrange the Temari Sushi on a serving platter.
Serve with soy sauce, wasabi, and pickled ginger on the side.

Tuna and Cucumber Temari Sush

Ingredients:

Sushi rice (short-grain Japanese rice)
Fresh tuna, thinly sliced
Cucumber, thinly sliced
Sesame seeds
Soy sauce, for dipping
Wasabi, for serving
Pickled ginger, for serving

Instructions:

Prepare the sushi rice by cooking it according to the package instructions. Once cooked, let it cool to room temperature.
Wet your hands with water to prevent the rice from sticking. Take a small amount of sushi rice and shape it into a compact ball using your palms. The rice ball should be around 1-2 inches in diameter.
Place a slice of tuna on top of the rice ball.
Add a slice of cucumber on top of the tuna.
Sprinkle some sesame seeds on top of the cucumber.
Repeat the process with the remaining ingredients to make more Temari Sushi balls.
Arrange the Temari Sushi on a serving platter.
Serve with soy sauce, wasabi, and pickled ginger on the side.
Feel free to experiment with different fillings and toppings for your Temari Sushi to create your own unique combinations. Enjoy the delightful and visually appealing Temari Sushi!

Sushi Bowls

Sushi bowls, also known as sushi rice bowls or poke bowls, are a popular and convenient way to enjoy the flavors of sushi without the need for rolling or shaping. Here's a recipe for a basic sushi bowl:

Ingredients:

2 cups sushi rice (short-grain Japanese rice)
4 tablespoons rice vinegar
2 tablespoons sugar
1 teaspoon salt
Assorted toppings (such as sashimi-grade fish, cooked shrimp, avocado, cucumber, edamame, seaweed salad, pickled ginger, etc.)
Soy sauce, for drizzling
Wasabi, for serving
Pickled ginger, for serving

Instructions:

Cook the sushi rice according to the package instructions. Once cooked, transfer it to a large bowl. In a small bowl, mix together the rice vinegar, sugar, and salt until the sugar and salt dissolve.

While the rice is still warm, pour the vinegar mixture over the rice. Gently fold and mix the rice using a wooden spatula or rice paddle, ensuring that the vinegar is evenly distributed. Let the rice cool to room temperature.

Prepare your desired toppings by slicing or cutting them into bite-sized pieces. Some popular choices include sashimi-grade fish like salmon, tuna, or yellowtail, cooked shrimp, avocado, cucumber, edamame, seaweed salad, pickled ginger, and more.

To assemble the sushi bowls, start with a generous scoop of sushi rice in each bowl.

Arrange the assorted toppings over the rice, placing them in separate sections or mixing them together, based on your preference.

Drizzle some soy sauce over the toppings for added flavor. You can also add a small amount of wasabi for heat and serve pickled ginger on the side for a palate cleanser.

Serve the sushi bowls immediately and enjoy!

You can customize your sushi bowls with your favorite ingredients and toppings. Get creative and build your own unique combinations for a delicious and satisfying meal.

Sushi Burrito

Sushi burritos are a fusion of Japanese sushi and Mexican burritos, offering a convenient and flavorful way to enjoy sushi fillings wrapped in a large sheet of seaweed. Here's a recipe for a sushi burrito:

Ingredients:

Sushi rice (short-grain Japanese rice)
Large sheets of seaweed (nori)
Assorted fillings (such as sashimi-grade fish, cooked shrimp, avocado, cucumber, carrots, sprouts, etc.)
Soy sauce, for dipping
Wasabi, for serving
Pickled ginger, for serving

Instructions:

Cook the sushi rice according to the package instructions. Once cooked, let it cool to room temperature.
Lay a sheet of seaweed (nori) on a clean and dry surface.
Wet your hands with water to prevent the rice from sticking. Take a handful of sushi rice and spread it evenly over the seaweed, leaving a small border at the edges.
Arrange your desired fillings in a line across the center of the rice, leaving some space at the top and bottom.
Starting from one end, tightly roll the seaweed and rice around the fillings, applying gentle pressure to ensure it holds together.
Once rolled, use a sharp knife to cut the sushi burrito in half or into smaller, handheld portions.
Repeat the process with the remaining ingredients to make more sushi burritos.
Serve the sushi burritos with soy sauce, wasabi, and pickled ginger on the side.
Sushi burritos are versatile, and you can customize them with a variety of fillings and sauces according to your taste preferences. They make a great portable meal or snack option. Enjoy the fusion flavors and unique presentation of sushi burritos!

Sushi Tacos

Sushi tacos are a creative and delicious fusion of Japanese sushi and Mexican tacos. They typically feature sushi ingredients and fillings served in a crispy taco shell. Here's a recipe for sushi tacos:

Ingredients:

Sushi rice (short-grain Japanese rice)
Nori sheets (seaweed), cut into small rectangles
Assorted sushi fillings (such as sashimi-grade fish, cooked shrimp, avocado, cucumber, carrots, sprouts, etc.)
Crispy taco shells
Soy sauce, for drizzling
Wasabi, for serving
Pickled ginger, for serving

Instructions:

Prepare the sushi rice by cooking it according to the package instructions. Once cooked, let it cool to room temperature.

Wet your hands with water to prevent the rice from sticking. Take a small amount of sushi rice and shape it into a rectangular strip or ball that will fit inside the taco shell.
Place a small piece of nori sheet on the bottom of the taco shell to act as a base.
Fill the taco shell with your desired sushi fillings, such as sashimi-grade fish, cooked shrimp, avocado, cucumber, carrots, sprouts, or any other ingredients you enjoy.
Top the fillings with the shaped sushi rice, pressing it gently to hold everything together.
Drizzle some soy sauce over the fillings for added flavor.
Repeat the process with the remaining taco shells and fillings.
Serve the sushi tacos immediately, garnished with wasabi and pickled ginger on the side.
Sushi tacos allow for endless creativity, so feel free to experiment with different combinations of fillings and sauces to suit your taste preferences. Enjoy the unique fusion of flavors and textures that sushi tacos offer!

Inari Sushi

Inari sushi is a type of sushi that consists of sushi rice wrapped in sweet and savory seasoned tofu pouches. It is a popular and delightful dish in Japanese cuisine. Here's a recipe for inari sushi:

Ingredients:

2 cups sushi rice (short-grain Japanese rice)
4 cups water
8 inari-age (seasoned tofu pouches), available at Asian grocery stores
1/4 cup soy sauce
1/4 cup mirin (sweet rice wine)
1 tablespoon sugar
Optional toppings: sesame seeds, sliced scallions, pickled ginger

Instructions:

Rinse the sushi rice under cold water until the water runs clear. Drain the rice.

In a rice cooker or saucepan, cook the sushi rice with water according to the package instructions. Once cooked, let it cool slightly.
In a separate saucepan, combine the soy sauce, mirin, and sugar. Heat over medium heat until the sugar has dissolved and the mixture is well combined.
Place the inari-age (seasoned tofu pouches) in the soy sauce mixture, making sure they are fully submerged. Simmer for about 5 minutes to allow the pouches to absorb the flavors.
Remove the tofu pouches from the saucepan and gently squeeze out any excess liquid.
Open each tofu pouch carefully to form a pocket. Fill each pouch with a scoop of sushi rice, gently pressing it in to fill the pouch completely.
Optional: Garnish the inari sushi with sesame seeds, sliced scallions, or pickled ginger for added flavor and presentation.
Serve the inari sushi at room temperature or chilled.
Inari sushi is a versatile dish, and you can customize it by adding additional fillings such as vegetables or seafood to the rice before filling the tofu pouches. Enjoy the sweet and savory flavors of this delightful sushi variation!

Las Vegas Roll

The Las Vegas Roll is a popular sushi roll that originated in the United States. It typically features a combination of ingredients such as salmon, cream cheese, avocado, and a tempura-style batter. Here's a recipe for the Las Vegas Roll:

Ingredients:

4 sheets of nori (seaweed)
2 cups sushi rice (short-grain Japanese rice)
4 ounces cream cheese, cut into thin strips
8 ounces fresh salmon, sliced into thin strips
1 ripe avocado, sliced into thin strips
Tempura batter mix (available at most grocery stores)
Vegetable oil, for frying
Soy sauce, for serving
Wasabi, for serving
Pickled ginger, for serving

Instructions:

Cook the sushi rice according to the package instructions. Once cooked, let it cool to room temperature.

Lay a sheet of nori on a bamboo sushi mat or a clean surface.

Wet your hands with water to prevent the rice from sticking. Take a handful of sushi rice and spread it evenly over the nori, leaving a small border at the top and bottom edges.
Place strips of cream cheese, salmon, and avocado horizontally across the rice, about 1 inch from the bottom edge.
Starting from the bottom edge, tightly roll the nori and rice over the fillings, using the sushi mat to help create a compact roll.
In a small bowl, prepare the tempura batter mix according to the package instructions.
Heat vegetable oil in a deep frying pan or pot to approximately 350°F (175°C).
Dip the entire Las Vegas roll into the prepared tempura batter, ensuring it is evenly coated.
Carefully place the battered roll into the hot oil and fry until the tempura batter turns golden brown and crispy. This should take about 2-3 minutes.
Remove the fried roll from the oil and let it cool slightly. Using a sharp knife, slice the roll into bite-sized pieces.
Serve the Las Vegas Roll with soy sauce, wasabi, and pickled ginger on the side.
The Las Vegas Roll is a unique and indulgent sushi roll that combines different flavors and textures. Enjoy the crispy exterior and creamy filling of this delicious sushi variation!

Spam Musubi

Spam Musubi is a popular Hawaiian snack that features a slice of grilled spam on top of a block of rice, wrapped with a strip of nori (seaweed). It's a delicious and satisfying treat. Here's a recipe for Spam Musubi:

Ingredients:

2 cups sushi rice (short-grain Japanese rice)
4 cups water
1 can of spam
4 sheets of nori (seaweed), cut into strips
Soy sauce, for brushing
Furikake (Japanese rice seasoning), optional

Instructions:

Rinse the sushi rice under cold water until the water runs clear. Drain the rice.
In a rice cooker or saucepan, cook the sushi rice with water according to the package instructions. Once cooked, let it cool slightly.

While the rice is cooking, open the can of spam and slice it into 1/4-inch thick slices.
In a skillet or frying pan, cook the spam slices over medium heat until they are browned and slightly crispy on each side. Remove from the heat and set aside.
Wet your hands with water to prevent the rice from sticking. Take a handful of sushi rice and shape it into a rectangular block that is roughly the same size as the spam slices.
Brush one side of each spam slice with soy sauce for added flavor.
Place a slice of spam on top of each rice block.
Wrap a strip of nori around the rice and spam, securing it in place. The nori should act as a band to hold everything together.
Optional: Sprinkle furikake (Japanese rice seasoning) over the rice for additional flavor and visual appeal.
Repeat the process with the remaining rice, spam, and nori.
Serve the Spam Musubi at room temperature or chilled. You can individually wrap each musubi in plastic wrap for easy transport or storage.
Spam Musubi is a delightful snack that can be enjoyed on its own or as part of a larger meal. It's a favorite among locals and visitors in Hawaii. Enjoy the unique combination of flavors and textures in this tasty treat!

Dragon Roll

The Dragon Roll is a popular sushi roll that typically features eel, avocado, and cucumber. It is then topped with thinly sliced avocado to resemble the scales of a dragon. Here's a recipe for the Dragon Roll:

Ingredients:

4 sheets of nori (seaweed)
2 cups sushi rice (short-grain Japanese rice)
8 ounces cooked eel, sliced into thin strips
1 avocado, sliced into thin strips
1/2 cucumber, peeled and sliced into thin strips
Soy sauce, for dipping
Wasabi, for serving
Pickled ginger, for serving
Toasted sesame seeds, for garnish

Instructions:

Cook the sushi rice according to the package instructions. Once cooked, let it cool to room temperature.
Lay a sheet of nori on a bamboo sushi mat or a clean surface.
Wet your hands with water to prevent the rice from sticking. Take a handful of sushi rice and spread it evenly over the nori, leaving a small border at the top and bottom edges.
Place strips of eel, avocado, and cucumber horizontally across the rice, about 1 inch from the bottom edge.
Starting from the bottom edge, tightly roll the nori and rice over the fillings, using the sushi mat to help create a compact roll.
Optional: Spread a thin layer of toasted sesame seeds on top of the sushi roll. This will add texture and flavor.
Place a sheet of plastic wrap over the sushi roll and gently press down to shape and tighten the roll. This will help keep the ingredients in place when slicing.
Remove the plastic wrap and transfer the sushi roll to a cutting board. Using a sharp knife, slice the roll into bite-sized pieces.
Arrange the sliced Dragon Roll on a serving plate.
Garnish the top of each sushi piece with thinly sliced avocado, resembling the scales of a dragon.
Serve the Dragon Roll with soy sauce, wasabi, and pickled ginger on the side.
The Dragon Roll is a visually appealing and delicious sushi roll that is sure to impress. Enjoy the combination of flavors and textures in this delightful creation!

Sushi Ginger

Sushi ginger, also known as Gari, is the pickled ginger that is commonly served alongside sushi. It is used as a palate cleanser between different types of sushi or as a condiment to add a refreshing and tangy flavor to sushi rolls. Here's a recipe for sushi ginger:

Ingredients:

Fresh ginger root (about 200 grams)
1 cup rice vinegar
1/2 cup sugar
1 teaspoon salt

Instructions:

Peel the ginger root using a spoon or a peeler to remove the outer skin.

Slice the ginger into very thin slices. You can use a mandoline slicer or a sharp knife to achieve thin and even slices.

Place the sliced ginger in a bowl and sprinkle the salt over it. Let it sit for about 30 minutes to draw out excess moisture.

In a small saucepan, combine the rice vinegar and sugar. Heat the mixture over medium heat, stirring occasionally, until the sugar is completely dissolved.

Once the sugar has dissolved, remove the saucepan from heat and let the vinegar mixture cool to room temperature.

After the ginger has been sitting for 30 minutes, use your hands or a clean cloth to squeeze out the excess moisture from the ginger slices.

Place the ginger slices into a sterilized glass jar or container.

Pour the cooled vinegar mixture over the ginger slices, ensuring that all the ginger is submerged in the liquid.

Seal the jar or container tightly and refrigerate for at least 24 hours before using. The longer the ginger sits in the pickling liquid, the more flavorful it will become.

Sushi ginger can be stored in the refrigerator for several months.

Sushi ginger adds a tangy and refreshing element to sushi dishes. It is commonly enjoyed alongside sushi rolls, sashimi, or nigiri sushi. Enjoy the homemade sushi ginger with your favorite sushi creations!

Hosomaki (Thin Sushi Roll)

Hosomaki is a type of thin sushi roll that typically contains only one ingredient as the filling. It is a simple and classic sushi roll that is easy to make at home. Here's a recipe for Hosomaki:

Ingredients:

2 sheets of nori (seaweed)
1 cup sushi rice (short-grain Japanese rice)
Your choice of filling (such as cucumber, avocado, cooked shrimp, or smoked salmon)
Soy sauce, for dipping
Wasabi, for serving
Pickled ginger, for serving

Instructions:

Cook the sushi rice according to the package instructions. Once cooked, let it cool to room temperature.

Place a sheet of nori on a bamboo sushi mat or a clean surface.
Wet your hands with water to prevent the rice from sticking. Take half of the sushi rice and spread it evenly over the nori, leaving a small border at the top edge.
Place a thin strip of your chosen filling horizontally across the rice, about 1 inch from the bottom edge.
Starting from the bottom edge, tightly roll the nori and rice over the filling, using the sushi mat to help create a compact roll. Apply gentle pressure as you roll to ensure a firm and tight roll.
Wet the top edge of the nori sheet with a bit of water to seal the roll.
Repeat the process with the remaining nori sheet, rice, and filling.
Using a sharp knife, slice each roll into bite-sized pieces, about 1 inch thick.
Serve the Hosomaki with soy sauce, wasabi, and pickled ginger on the side.
Hosomaki is a versatile sushi roll, and you can experiment with different fillings to suit your taste preferences. Enjoy the simplicity and flavors of this traditional thin sushi roll!

Futomaki (Fat Sushi Roll)

Futomaki is a type of thick sushi roll that typically contains multiple ingredients as the filling. It is a hearty and flavorful sushi roll that is great for those who prefer a more substantial sushi option. Here's a recipe for Futomaki:

Ingredients:

2 sheets of nori (seaweed)
2 cups sushi rice (short-grain Japanese rice)
Your choice of fillings (such as cooked shrimp, crab sticks, cucumber, avocado, tamagoyaki, and pickled vegetables)
Soy sauce, for dipping
Wasabi, for serving
Pickled ginger, for serving

Instructions:

Cook the sushi rice according to the package instructions. Once cooked, let it cool to room temperature.

Place a sheet of nori on a bamboo sushi mat or a clean surface.
Wet your hands with water to prevent the rice from sticking. Take half of the sushi rice and spread it evenly over the nori, leaving a small border at the top edge.
Arrange your choice of fillings horizontally across the rice, about 1 inch from the bottom edge.
Starting from the bottom edge, tightly roll the nori and rice over the fillings, using the sushi mat to help create a compact roll. Apply gentle pressure as you roll to ensure a firm and tight roll.
Wet the top edge of the nori sheet with a bit of water to seal the roll.
Repeat the process with the remaining nori sheet, rice, and fillings.
Using a sharp knife, slice each roll into bite-sized pieces, about 1 inch thick.
Serve the Futomaki with soy sauce, wasabi, and pickled ginger on the side.
Futomaki allows for creativity and variety with its multiple fillings. You can customize the fillings based on your preferences and create a colorful and flavorful sushi roll. Enjoy the deliciousness of this satisfying fat sushi roll!

Sushi Maki

Sushi Maki refers to any type of sushi roll that is made by wrapping rice and fillings with a sheet of nori (seaweed). It is a versatile and customizable style of sushi that can accommodate a wide range of ingredients. Here's a basic recipe for making sushi Maki:

Ingredients:

Sushi rice (short-grain Japanese rice)
Nori sheets (seaweed)
Assorted fillings (examples: raw or cooked fish, shrimp, crab sticks, cucumber, avocado, carrots, cream cheese, etc.)
Soy sauce, for dipping
Wasabi, for serving
Pickled ginger, for serving

Instructions:

Prepare the sushi rice by cooking it according to the package instructions. Once cooked, let it cool to room temperature.

Lay a sheet of nori on a bamboo sushi mat or a clean surface.
Wet your hands with water to prevent the rice from sticking. Take a handful of sushi rice and spread it evenly over the nori, leaving a small border at the top edge.

Arrange your choice of fillings horizontally across the rice, about 1 inch from the bottom edge
Starting from the bottom edge, tightly roll the nori and rice over the fillings, using the sushi mat to help create a compact roll. Apply gentle pressure as you roll to ensure a firm and tight roll.
Wet the top edge of the nori sheet with a bit of water to seal the roll.
Repeat the process with additional nori sheets, rice, and fillings to make more sushi rolls.
Using a sharp knife, slice each roll into bite-sized pieces, about 1 inch thick.
Serve the sushi Maki with soy sauce, wasabi, and pickled ginger on the side.
Sushi Maki is a versatile and customizable sushi style, and you can get creative with your choice of fillings to suit your taste preferences. Enjoy the process of rolling and creating your own delicious sushi Maki!

Uramaki

Uramaki, also known as inside-out rolls, is a type of sushi roll where the rice is on the outside, and the nori (seaweed) is on the inside, wrapped around the filling. Uramaki rolls often have a variety of fillings and are typically coated in sesame seeds or tobiko (flying fish roe) for added flavor and texture. Here's a recipe for Uramaki:

Ingredients:

Sushi rice (short-grain Japanese rice)
Nori sheets (seaweed)
Assorted fillings (examples: crab sticks, cucumber, avocado, cooked shrimp, smoked salmon, etc.)
Toasted sesame seeds or tobiko (optional, for coating the rolls)
Soy sauce, for dipping
Wasabi, for serving
Pickled ginger, for serving

Instructions:

Prepare the sushi rice by cooking it according to the package instructions. Once cooked, let it cool to room temperature.

Lay a sheet of nori on a bamboo sushi mat or a clean surface.

Wet your hands with water to prevent the rice from sticking. Take a handful of sushi rice and spread it evenly over the entire surface of the nori sheet, leaving a small border around the edges.
Sprinkle a thin layer of toasted sesame seeds or tobiko over the rice, if desired.
Flip the nori sheet over so that the rice side is facing down on the sushi mat.
Arrange your choice of fillings horizontally across the nori sheet, about 1 inch from the bottom edge.
Starting from the bottom edge, tightly roll the nori and fillings over, using the sushi mat to help create a compact roll. Apply gentle pressure as you roll to ensure a firm and tight roll.
Wet the top edge of the nori sheet with a bit of water to seal the roll.
Repeat the process with additional nori sheets, rice, and fillings to make more Uramaki rolls.
Using a sharp knife, slice each roll into bite-sized pieces, about 1 inch thick.
Serve the Uramaki rolls with soy sauce, wasabi, and pickled ginger on the side.
Uramaki rolls offer endless possibilities for fillings and toppings, so feel free to get creative and experiment with different combinations. Enjoy the unique flavors and textures of these inside-out sushi rolls!

Vegan Sushi

Here's a recipe for vegan sushi that omits animal-based ingredients and focuses on plant-based alternatives:

Ingredients:

Sushi rice (short-grain Japanese rice)
Nori sheets (seaweed)
Assorted vegetables (examples: cucumber, avocado, carrots, bell peppers, asparagus, sweet potato, etc.)
Vegan protein alternatives (examples: marinated tofu, tempeh, or mock crab sticks)
Soy sauce or tamari, for dipping
Wasabi, for serving
Pickled ginger, for serving

Instructions:

Cook the sushi rice according to the package instructions. Once cooked, let it cool to room temperature.

Prepare the vegetables by slicing them into thin strips or julienne cuts.
Lay a sheet of nori on a bamboo sushi mat or a clean surface.
Wet your hands with water to prevent the rice from sticking. Take a handful of sushi rice and spread it evenly over the entire surface of the nori sheet, leaving a small border around the edges.
Place the vegetable and vegan protein alternatives horizontally across the nori sheet, about 1 inch from the bottom edge.
Starting from the bottom edge, tightly roll the nori and fillings over, using the sushi mat to help create a compact roll. Apply gentle pressure as you roll to ensure a firm and tight roll.
Wet the top edge of the nori sheet with a bit of water to seal the roll.
Repeat the process with additional nori sheets, rice, and fillings to make more vegan sushi rolls.
Using a sharp knife, slice each roll into bite-sized pieces, about 1 inch thick.
Serve the vegan sushi rolls with soy sauce or tamari, wasabi, and pickled ginger on the side.
Feel free to get creative with your vegan sushi fillings and toppings. You can also experiment with different sauces, such as a vegan spicy mayo or a sesame ginger dressing, to add extra flavor.
Enjoy the plant-based goodness of vegan sushi!

Spider Roll

The Spider Roll is a popular sushi roll that typically features a tempura-fried soft-shell crab as the main ingredient. Here's a recipe for Spider Roll:

Ingredients:

4 sheets of nori (seaweed)
2 cups sushi rice (short-grain Japanese rice)
2 soft-shell crabs, cleaned and patted dry
Tempura batter mix
Vegetable oil, for frying
Assorted fillings (such as cucumber, avocado, or lettuce)
Soy sauce, for dipping
Wasabi, for serving
Pickled ginger, for serving

Instructions:

Cook the sushi rice according to the package instructions. Once cooked, let it cool to room temperature.

Prepare the tempura batter mix according to the package instructions.
Dip each soft-shell crab into the tempura batter, ensuring it is evenly coated.
Heat vegetable oil in a deep pan or pot to about 350°F (175°C). Carefully place the coated soft-shell crabs into the hot oil and fry them until golden brown and crispy, usually for about 3-4 minutes per side. Remove them from the oil and place them on a paper towel-lined plate to drain excess oil.
Lay a sheet of nori on a bamboo sushi mat or a clean surface.
Wet your hands with water to prevent the rice from sticking. Take a handful of sushi rice and spread it evenly over the entire surface of the nori sheet, leaving a small border around the edges.
Arrange your choice of fillings horizontally across the nori sheet, about 1 inch from the bottom edge.
Place the fried soft-shell crab on top of the fillings.
Starting from the bottom edge, tightly roll the nori and fillings over, using the sushi mat to help create a compact roll. Apply gentle pressure as you roll to ensure a firm and tight roll.
Wet the top edge of the nori sheet with a bit of water to seal the roll
Repeat the process with the remaining nori sheets, rice, fillings, and soft-shell crabs to make more Spider Rolls.
Using a sharp knife, slice each roll into bite-sized pieces, about 1 inch thick.
Serve the Spider Rolls with soy sauce, wasabi, and pickled ginger on the side.
The Spider Roll is a delicious and crispy sushi roll that offers a unique combination of flavors and textures. Enjoy the crunch of the tempura-fried soft-shell crab in this popular sushi creation!

King Crab Roll

The King Crab Roll is a luxurious sushi roll that features sweet and succulent king crab meat as the main ingredient. Here's a recipe for King Crab Roll:

Ingredients:

4 sheets of nori (seaweed)
2 cups sushi rice (short-grain Japanese rice)
8 ounces cooked king crab meat, shredded or sliced
1 avocado, sliced
Cucumber, thinly sliced
Mayonnaise or spicy mayo, for drizzling
Soy sauce, for dipping
Wasabi, for serving
Pickled ginger, for serving

Instructions:

Cook the sushi rice according to the package instructions. Once cooked, let it cool to room temperature.

Lay a sheet of nori on a bamboo sushi mat or a clean surface.
Wet your hands with water to prevent the rice from sticking. Take a handful of sushi rice and spread it evenly over the entire surface of the nori sheet, leaving a small border around the edges.
Place a layer of sliced avocado and cucumber on top of the rice, leaving some space at the top for rolling.
Add a generous amount of shredded or sliced king crab meat on top of the avocado and cucumber.
Drizzle mayonnaise or spicy mayo over the fillings.
Starting from the bottom edge, tightly roll the nori and fillings over, using the sushi mat to help create a compact roll. Apply gentle pressure as you roll to ensure a firm and tight roll.
Wet the top edge of the nori sheet with a bit of water to seal the roll.
Repeat the process with the remaining nori sheets, rice, and fillings to make more King Crab Rolls
Using a sharp knife, slice each roll into bite-sized pieces, about 1 inch thick.
Serve the King Crab Rolls with soy sauce, wasabi, and pickled ginger on the side.
The King Crab Roll is a decadent and flavorful sushi roll that highlights the delicate and rich taste of king crab. Enjoy the indulgence of this special sushi creation!

Alaska Roll

Ingredients:

4 sheets of nori seaweed
3 cups of sushi rice, cooked
8 oz of cooked Alaskan king crab meat, shredded
1 avocado, sliced
1/2 cucumber, sliced
2 green onions, thinly sliced
1 tbsp of toasted sesame seeds
Soy sauce, for serving
Wasabi, for serving
Pickled ginger, for serving

Instructions:

Lay a sheet of nori seaweed onto a sushi mat with the shiny side down.
Spread a thin layer of cooked sushi rice over the nori, leaving a small border at the top.
Place the shredded crab meat, avocado, cucumber, and green onions in a line across the center of the rice.
Sprinkle with sesame seeds.
Using the sushi mat, roll the nori tightly around the filling, using the border of rice to seal the roll.
Repeat with the remaining nori sheets and filling.
Slice each roll into 8 pieces using a sharp knife.
Serve with soy sauce, wasabi, and pickled ginger.
Enjoy your delicious Alaska Roll!

Octopus Sushi

Ingredients:

2 cups of sushi rice, cooked
1 small octopus (about 1 pound), cleaned and sliced into small pieces
1/4 cup of rice vinegar
1 tbsp of sugar
1 tsp of salt
Nori seaweed sheets
Wasabi paste
Soy sauce
Pickled ginger
Sesame seeds (optional)

Instructions:

In a bowl, mix together the rice vinegar, sugar, and salt until the sugar and salt dissolve.
Add the cooked sushi rice and mix well.
In a pot of boiling water, blanch the sliced octopus for 1 minute.
Drain and rinse the octopus under cold running water.
Cut the nori sheets in half.
Take a small amount of the seasoned sushi rice and shape it into a small ball.
Place a slice of octopus on top of the rice ball and wrap it with a half-sheet of nori seaweed.
Repeat until all of the rice and octopus are used up.
Serve the octopus sushi with wasabi paste, soy sauce, and pickled ginger.
Optional: sprinkle sesame seeds over the sushi for an extra crunch.
Enjoy your delicious octopus sushi!

Flying Tiger Sushi Roll

The Flying Tiger Sushi Roll is a popular sushi roll that features a unique combination of ingredients. Here's a recipe to make it at home:

Ingredients:

2 cups of sushi rice, cooked
4 sheets of nori seaweed
1/2 lb of cooked shrimp, sliced in half lengthwise
1/2 lb of cooked eel, sliced into thin strips
1 avocado, sliced
1/4 cup of mayonnaise
1 tbsp of sriracha sauce
1 tsp of honey
Salt, to taste
2 green onions, thinly sliced

Instructions:

In a small bowl, mix together the mayonnaise, sriracha sauce, honey, and salt to make the spicy mayo sauce.
Place a sheet of nori on a sushi mat.
Spread a thin layer of cooked sushi rice over the nori, leaving a 1-inch border at the top.
Spread a thin layer of the spicy mayo sauce over the rice.
Add a layer of sliced avocado, followed by a layer of cooked shrimp and eel strips.
Sprinkle some thinly sliced green onions on top of the ingredients.
Roll the sushi tightly using the sushi mat.
Repeat with the remaining ingredients.
Use a sharp knife to slice the sushi into bite-sized pieces.
Serve the Flying Tiger sushi roll with soy sauce and pickled ginger on the side.
Enjoy your delicious Flying Tiger sushi roll!

Dynamite Rolls

Ingredients:

1 cup sushi rice
1 1/4 cups water
2 tablespoons rice vinegar
1 tablespoon sugar
1/2 teaspoon salt
4 sheets of nori
8 cooked shrimp, peeled and deveined
1 avocado, thinly sliced
4 tablespoons spicy mayonnaise (mix 2 tablespoons mayonnaise with 2 teaspoons sriracha sauce)
1/4 cup chopped scallions
1 tablespoon toasted sesame seeds

Instructions:

Rinse the sushi rice several times with cold water until the water runs clear. Drain the rice and add it to a medium-sized pot with 1 1/4 cups of water. Bring the water to a boil, then reduce the heat to low, cover the pot with a tight-fitting lid, and let the rice simmer for 18-20 minutes.

While the rice is cooking, mix together the rice vinegar, sugar, and salt in a small bowl. Once the rice has finished cooking, transfer it to a large bowl, and pour the vinegar mixture over the rice. Mix well to combine, then set aside to cool.

Cut each sheet of nori in half crosswise, and place one half on a sushi mat with the shiny side facing down. Wet your hands with cold water and scoop about 1/4 cup of the cooled sushi rice onto the nori. Use your fingers to gently press the rice into an even layer, leaving a 1-inch border along the top edge of the nori.

Spread 1 tablespoon of the spicy mayonnaise on the rice, then add 2 shrimp and a few slices of avocado on top. Sprinkle some chopped scallions and toasted sesame seeds on top.

Use the sushi mat to tightly roll the nori around the filling, using the border at the top to seal the roll closed. Repeat with the remaining ingredients.

Use a sharp knife to cut each roll into 6-8 pieces. Serve immediately with extra spicy mayo and soy sauce for dipping. Enjoy your delicious dynamite rolls!

Crunchy Roll Sushi

Ingredients:

2 cups sushi rice
2 cups water
1/4 cup rice vinegar
1 tablespoon sugar
1 teaspoon salt
4 sheets of nori
1/2 cup panko bread crumbs
1 avocado, sliced
1/2 cucumber, sliced into matchsticks
8-10 cooked shrimp, sliced in half lengthwise
1 tablespoon spicy mayo (1/4 cup mayo mixed with 1 tablespoon Sriracha sauce)
Soy sauce, for dipping

Instructions:

Rinse the sushi rice in cold water until the water runs clear. In a medium saucepan, combine the rice and water and bring to a boil. Reduce the heat to low, cover, and cook for 18 minutes. Remove from heat and let sit for 10 minutes before fluffing with a fork.
In a small saucepan, heat the rice vinegar, sugar, and salt over low heat until the sugar and salt have dissolved.
Add the vinegar mixture to the rice and stir to combine.
Toast the panko bread crumbs in a dry pan over medium heat until golden brown.
Lay a sheet of nori shiny side down on a sushi mat. Spread a thin layer of sushi rice over the nori, leaving a 1-inch border at the top. Sprinkle the panko bread crumbs over the rice.
Arrange the avocado, cucumber, and shrimp on top of the bread crumbs. Drizzle with spicy mayo.
Using the sushi mat, roll the sushi tightly from the bottom up, using the 1-inch border of rice at the top to seal the roll.
Cut the sushi into 8-10 pieces and serve with soy sauce for dipping. Enjoy your Crunchy Roll Sushi!

Caterpillar Rolls

Ingredients:

2 cups sushi rice
2 tablespoons rice vinegar
2 tablespoons sugar
1 teaspoon salt
5 sheets nori
1 ripe avocado, peeled and sliced
1/2 cup unagi sauce
1/2 cup toasted sesame seeds
8 cooked shrimp, peeled and deveined
1/2 cup cucumber, julienned

Instructions:

Rinse sushi rice in cold water until the water runs clear. Add the rice and 2 1/4 cups water to a pot and bring to a boil. Reduce heat to low, cover, and simmer for 18 minutes. Remove from heat and let sit for 10 minutes.

In a small saucepan, combine the rice vinegar, sugar, and salt. Heat over low heat, stirring occasionally, until the sugar and salt have dissolved. Remove from heat and let cool.

Spread the cooked sushi rice onto a baking sheet and sprinkle the cooled vinegar mixture over the rice. Use a wooden spoon to mix the rice, being careful not to break the grains.

Place a sheet of nori onto a bamboo mat with the shiny side facing down. Wet your hands with water and grab a handful of rice. Spread the rice onto the nori, leaving a 1/2-inch border at the top. Sprinkle the sesame seeds over the rice, pressing lightly to make them stick.

Flip the nori over so that the rice is facing down. Place the sliced avocado onto the nori, followed by the cooked shrimp and cucumber.

Roll the sushi tightly, using the bamboo mat to help you. Roll until the seam is on the bottom. Cut the sushi into 8 equal pieces. Drizzle the unagi sauce over the top of the sushi and serve.

Surf and Turf Roll

Ingredients:

1 lb. cooked shrimp, peeled and deveined
1/2 lb. cooked beef tenderloin, sliced into thin strips
4 sheets of nori seaweed
4 cups sushi rice, cooked
2 tbsp rice vinegar
1 tbsp sugar
1 tsp salt
1 avocado, sliced
1/4 cup mayonnaise
1 tbsp sriracha sauce
1/4 cup eel sauce
1/4 cup tobiko (flying fish roe)
1/4 cup chopped green onions
Wasabi and soy sauce, for serving

Instructions:

In a small bowl, mix together the rice vinegar, sugar, and salt. Add this mixture to the cooked sushi rice and stir until well combined.

Lay a sheet of nori on a bamboo sushi mat, shiny side down. Spread a thin layer of the prepared sushi rice over the nori, leaving a 1-inch border at the top.

Arrange slices of beef and shrimp over the rice, then add a layer of sliced avocado on top.

In a small bowl, mix together the mayonnaise and sriracha sauce. Drizzle this over the top of the avocado layer.

Using the sushi mat, tightly roll the nori into a cylinder, making sure to tuck in the filling as you go.

Slice the roll into 8 equal pieces and place them on a serving platter.

Drizzle the eel sauce over the top of the rolls, then sprinkle with tobiko and chopped green onions.

Serve the rolls with wasabi and soy sauce on the side for dipping. Enjoy your Surf and Turf Roll!

Burning Volcano Sushi Roll with Lava Topping

Ingredients:

4 sheets of nori seaweed
4 cups of prepared sushi rice
4 oz. of sushi-grade salmon, thinly sliced
4 oz. of sushi-grade tuna, thinly sliced
1/2 an avocado, thinly sliced
1/4 cup of chopped green onion
1/4 cup of mayonnaise
1 tbsp. of sriracha
1 tbsp. of soy sauce
1 tbsp. of sesame oil
1/4 cup of tempura flakes
1/4 cup of tobiko (flying fish roe)
1/4 cup of masago (capelin roe)
1/4 cup of thinly sliced red cabbage
1/4 cup of thinly sliced carrots

For the Lava Topping:

1/2 cup of mayonnaise
1/4 cup of sriracha
1 tsp. of sesame oil
1 tsp. of honey

Instructions:

In a small bowl, mix together the mayonnaise, sriracha, soy sauce, and sesame oil to make the spicy mayo sauce. Set aside.
Place a sheet of nori on a sushi mat with the shiny side facing down.
Using damp hands, take a handful of sushi rice and spread it evenly over the nori, leaving a 1-inch border at the top.
Sprinkle some tempura flakes on top of the rice, followed by some green onion.
Flip the nori sheet over so that the rice is facing down on the mat.
Arrange the salmon, tuna, and avocado on top of the nori, leaving a 1-inch border at the top.
Roll the sushi tightly using the sushi mat, making sure to keep the fillings inside.
Using a sharp knife, cut the sushi roll into 8 pieces.
In a small bowl, mix together the mayonnaise, sriracha, sesame oil, and honey to make the lava topping.
Place the sushi pieces on a serving plate and top each piece with a dollop of the lava topping.
Sprinkle some tobiko and masago on top of the sushi pieces, followed by some thinly sliced red cabbage and carrots.
Serve immediately and enjoy your delicious Burning Volcano Sushi Roll with Lava Topping!

Teriyaki Chicken Sushi Roll

Ingredients:

2 cups of sushi rice
2 cups of water
1/4 cup of rice vinegar
2 tablespoons of sugar
1 teaspoon of salt
2 chicken breasts, sliced into thin strips
1/2 cup of teriyaki sauce
4 sheets of nori
1 avocado, sliced
1/2 cup of cucumber, sliced into thin strips
Sesame seeds, for garnish

Instructions:

Rinse the sushi rice in a strainer until the water runs clear. Then, add the rice and water to a rice cooker and cook according to the manufacturer's instructions. If you don't have a rice cooker, cook the rice in a saucepan over medium heat for about 18-20 minutes, or until the water has been absorbed and the rice is tender.

While the rice is cooking, make the teriyaki chicken. In a large pan, add the chicken strips and teriyaki sauce. Cook over medium-high heat until the chicken is fully cooked, and the sauce has thickened, about 8-10 minutes.

Once the rice is done cooking, transfer it to a large mixing bowl. In a small saucepan, heat the rice vinegar, sugar, and salt over low heat until the sugar has dissolved. Then, pour the mixture over the rice and stir well to combine.

To assemble the sushi rolls, place a sheet of nori on a sushi mat. Wet your hands with water, and then spread a layer of rice over the nori, leaving a 1-inch border at the top. Place a few slices of avocado and cucumber in a line across the center of the rice. Then, add a few pieces of teriyaki chicken on top of the vegetables.

Using the sushi mat, roll the sushi tightly from the bottom up, using the border of rice at the top to seal the roll. Repeat this process with the remaining nori and ingredients.

Slice the sushi rolls into bite-sized pieces, and then garnish with sesame seeds.

Enjoy your homemade Teriyaki Chicken Sushi Rolls!

Unagi Sushi Rolls

Ingredients:

1 cup sushi rice
1 1/4 cups water
2 tbsp rice vinegar
1 tbsp sugar
1/2 tsp salt
2 unagi fillets
1 tbsp soy sauce
1 tbsp mirin
1 tbsp sake
1 tsp sugar
1 tsp honey
2 sheets of nori
1/2 cucumber, peeled and cut into thin strips
Wasabi paste
Pickled ginger

Instructions:

Rinse the sushi rice in a fine mesh strainer until the water runs clear. Add the rice to a medium-sized saucepan and add water. Bring the water to a boil, reduce heat to low, cover the pan, and let simmer for 18-20 minutes or until the rice is cooked and tender.

In a small saucepan, combine the rice vinegar, sugar, and salt. Heat over low heat, stirring constantly until the sugar and salt are dissolved. Once dissolved, remove from heat and let cool.

Once the rice is done, transfer it to a large mixing bowl. Add the vinegar mixture and stir until well combined. Allow the rice to cool down to room temperature.

In a small saucepan, combine the soy sauce, mirin, sake, sugar, and honey. Heat over medium heat and bring to a boil. Reduce heat to low and simmer until the sauce is thickened and reduced by half.

Preheat your oven to 350°F. Place the unagi fillets on a baking sheet and brush with the sauce. Bake for 8-10 minutes, or until the unagi is cooked through.

Cut the cucumber into thin strips.

Place a sheet of nori on a bamboo sushi rolling mat, with the shiny side facing down. Spread a thin layer of wasabi paste over the nori. Spoon a small amount of sushi rice onto the nori and spread it out evenly, leaving a 1-inch border at the top.

Cut the unagi fillets into strips and arrange them in the center of the rice. Add the cucumber strips on top of the unagi.

Using the bamboo mat, roll up the sushi, making sure it is tightly packed. Wet the top border of the nori with water to seal the roll.

Using a sharp knife, cut the sushi roll into 8-10 pieces.

Serve the unagi sushi rolls with pickled ginger and additional soy sauce on the side.

Enjoy your delicious Unagi Sushi Rolls!

Fire Cracker Roll

Ingredients:

6 sheets of nori seaweed
3 cups of sushi rice
1 lb tempura shrimp
1 avocado, thinly sliced
1 cucumber, thinly sliced
1/4 cup mayonnaise
1/4 cup sriracha sauce
1 tbsp soy sauce
1 tbsp rice vinegar
1 tsp sugar
1 tsp salt

Instructions:

Cook the sushi rice according to the package instructions and set aside to cool.
Mix the mayonnaise, sriracha sauce, soy sauce, rice vinegar, sugar, and salt together in a small bowl to make the spicy mayo sauce.
Cut the tempura shrimp into halves.
Lay a sheet of nori on a sushi mat, shiny side down.
Wet your hands with water and scoop a handful of rice onto the nori.
Spread the rice evenly over the nori, leaving a 1-inch gap at the top.
Place the sliced cucumber and avocado on top of the rice.
Add the tempura shrimp on top of the cucumber and avocado.
Roll the sushi tightly using the sushi mat, making sure to tuck in the filling tightly.
Use a sharp knife to cut the sushi roll into bite-sized pieces.
Drizzle the spicy mayo sauce on top of the sushi roll and serve.
Enjoy your delicious Firecracker Roll!

Golden Avocado Sushi Roll

Ingredients:

2 cups sushi rice
2 cups water
1/4 cup rice vinegar
2 tablespoons sugar
1 tablespoon salt
4 sheets of nori
1 avocado, thinly sliced
1/2 cup tempura flakes
1/2 cup masago (fish roe)
1/2 cup sliced green onions
2 tablespoons mayonnaise
1 tablespoon sriracha hot sauce

Instructions:

Rinse the sushi rice with water until the water runs clear. Place the rice and water in a rice cooker and cook according to the manufacturer's instructions.
While the rice is cooking, mix together the rice vinegar, sugar, and salt in a small saucepan over low heat until the sugar and salt dissolve. Remove from heat and let cool.
When the rice is done cooking, transfer it to a large mixing bowl and add the vinegar mixture. Mix well to combine.
Lay a sheet of nori on a sushi mat or a piece of plastic wrap. Wet your hands with water and grab a handful of rice, spreading it evenly over the nori, leaving a 1-inch border at the top edge.
Arrange a few slices of avocado on top of the rice, then sprinkle some tempura flakes, masago, and green onions on top.
Roll the sushi tightly, using the mat or plastic wrap to help you. Seal the roll by moistening the border of the nori with water.
Repeat with the remaining ingredients to make 3 more sushi rolls.
In a small bowl, mix together the mayonnaise and sriracha hot sauce.
Slice the sushi rolls into bite-sized pieces and arrange them on a serving platter. Drizzle the spicy mayonnaise over the top of the sushi rolls.
Serve the Golden Avocado Sushi Rolls immediately and enjoy!

Tuna Mayo Sushi Rolls

Ingredients:

2 cups sushi rice
2 tablespoons rice vinegar
2 tablespoons sugar
1 tablespoon salt
4 sheets nori seaweed
1 can tuna, drained
2 tablespoons mayonnaise
1 avocado, sliced
1 cucumber, sliced
Wasabi, soy sauce, and pickled ginger for serving

Instructions:

Cook the sushi rice according to package instructions, then let it cool.
In a small saucepan, combine the rice vinegar, sugar, and salt. Heat over low heat, stirring until the sugar and salt dissolve. Once the mixture is cool, pour it over the sushi rice and mix well.
In a small bowl, mix the drained tuna and mayonnaise together.
Lay a sheet of nori on a bamboo sushi mat with the shiny side facing down.
Spread about ½ cup of sushi rice evenly over the nori, leaving a 1-inch border at the top edge.
Spread a thin layer of the tuna and mayonnaise mixture over the rice, then add a layer of sliced avocado and cucumber.
Roll up the sushi tightly, using the mat to help you. Wet the top border of the nori sheet with a little water to help it stick.
Repeat with the remaining nori sheets and filling.
Slice each sushi roll into bite-sized pieces with a sharp, wet knife.
Serve with wasabi, soy sauce, and pickled ginger.
Enjoy your Tuna Mayo Sushi Rolls!

Chumaki Rolls

Chumaki is a type of sushi roll that is characterized by its medium size and the use of a single filling. Here's a recipe for Chumaki Rolls:

Ingredients:

1 cup sushi rice
1 1/4 cups water
2 tablespoons rice vinegar
1 tablespoon sugar
1 teaspoon salt
4 sheets of nori
4 fillings (such as crab sticks, cooked shrimp, avocado, or cucumber)

Instructions:

Rinse the sushi rice in cold water until the water runs clear. Drain and add to a pot with 1 1/4 cups of water. Bring to a boil, then reduce heat to low, cover and simmer for 15 minutes. Turn off heat and let sit for another 10 minutes.
In a small saucepan, heat rice vinegar, sugar and salt until sugar and salt are dissolved.
Transfer the cooked rice to a large bowl and add the vinegar mixture. Use a spatula to mix until the rice is coated and let cool to room temperature.
Place a sheet of nori shiny side down on a sushi mat. With damp fingers, spread a thin layer of rice over the nori leaving a 1-inch border on the top edge.
Add a single filling in a horizontal line across the center of the rice
Use the sushi mat to tightly roll the sushi away from you. Lift the edge of the mat closest to you and roll it away from the sushi, pressing gently to form a tight roll.
Repeat with remaining nori sheets and fillings.
Use a sharp knife to slice each roll into 6-8 pieces.
Serve with soy sauce and pickled ginger.
Enjoy your homemade Chumaki Rolls!

Tamago Maki

Ingredients:

3 eggs
1 tablespoon sugar
1/2 teaspoon salt
1 tablespoon mirin (sweet cooking sake)
1 tablespoon vegetable oil
2 cups sushi rice
2 tablespoons rice vinegar
1 tablespoon sugar
1/2 teaspoon salt
2 sheets of nori (dried seaweed)

Instructions:

Start by making the sushi rice. Rinse the rice in a fine mesh strainer and place it in a large pot with 2 cups of water. Bring to a boil, then reduce the heat to low, cover, and cook for 15-20 minutes until the rice is tender and the water has been absorbed.
In a small bowl, mix together the rice vinegar, sugar, and salt until the sugar has dissolved. When the rice is done cooking, transfer it to a large bowl and drizzle the vinegar mixture over it. Gently mix the rice with a wooden spoon or spatula until the vinegar has been evenly distributed. Let the rice cool to room temperature.
In a separate bowl, whisk together the eggs, sugar, salt, and mirin until well combined.
Heat a non-stick skillet over medium-low heat and add the vegetable oil. When the oil is hot, pour in the egg mixture and cook for a few minutes until the bottom is set.
Use a spatula to flip the egg over and cook for another minute or so on the other side. Transfer the cooked egg to a plate and repeat with the remaining egg mixture.
Cut the egg into thin strips and set aside.
Lay a sheet of nori on a bamboo sushi mat, shiny side down. Spread a thin layer of sushi rice evenly over the nori, leaving about 1/2 inch of space at the top.
Arrange the egg strips in a row across the center of the rice.
Use the mat to roll the sushi tightly, pressing down gently as you go. Dampen the top edge of the nori with a bit of water to help seal the roll.
Repeat with the remaining nori, rice, and egg strips.
Slice the sushi rolls into pieces with a sharp knife, wiping the blade clean between cuts.
Serve with soy sauce, wasabi, and pickled ginger on the side.
Enjoy your delicious Tamago Maki!

I want to take a moment to express my heartfelt gratitude for your recent purchase of my recipe book. As a passionate food lover, nothing makes me happier than sharing my favorite recipes with others. Your decision to invest in my book not only supports my dream, but also shows your commitment to expanding your culinary horizons.

I sincerely hope that the recipes in the book will inspire you to try new things and add some excitement to your meals.

Thank you again for your support and for being a part of this journey with me. I hope my book will bring you many happy and delicious moments in the kitchen.

www.ingramcontent.com/pod-product-compliance
Lightning Source LLC
Chambersburg PA
CBHW081237080526
44587CB00022B/3966